Girl Pirates on the High Seas

Booty

by Sara Lorimer

ILLUSTRATIONS BY SUSAN SYNARSKI

BARNES
& NOBLE
BOOKS
NEW YORK

Acknowledgments

Thanks to Steve Mockus and Jodi Davis at Chronicle Books for guidance and good humor; Michelle Montgomery, Justine Kenin, and Lee Gillette for free-flowing grog and discussion; Patricia O'Toole, Lis Harris, and Richard Locke for launching the voyage; the contributors to Tony Malesic's *Pirates* e-mail list for sharing their enthusiasm and knowledge; and Lois Lorimer and Oliver Moffat, for everything.

This edition published in 2005 by Chronicle Books LLC exclusively for Barnes & Noble, Inc.

Text copyright © 2002 by Sara Lorimer.
Illustrations copyright © 2002 by Susan Synarski.

The Library of Congress has cataloged the previous edition [ISBN: 0-8118-3237-6]. Cataloging-in-Publication Data available.

ISBN 0-7607-7017-4

Manufactured in China.

Designed by Pamela Geismar
Typeset using Hoefler Fell Type Roman and Vitrina

10 9 8 7 6 5 4 3 2 1

Contents

Introduction

"They offered war rather than kisses . . ."
—Saxo Grammaticus

For as long as ships have sailed the seas there have been pirates. And for as long as there have been pirates, some of those pirates have been women.

And why not? Piracy offered everything to a woman that was denied her on land. At sea she had freedom and autonomy. She kept her own hours and spent them playing cards, drinking, gambling, sailing, eating, killing, and plundering. No household to run, no family to support, no chamber pots to empty. No arranged marriages, churchgoing, or financial dependency. Some of the women profiled here followed their lovers into piracy, others turned mercenary after a cross-dressing stint in the military, still others were born into piracy and carried out the family tradition. Fanny Campbell led a mutiny to find her fiancé; bizarre twists of fate landed Charlotte de Berry and Mary Read at sea; and Cheng I Sao turned pirate to escape a grim life of prostitution.

Their role in traditionally male pirate lore is that of freakish curiosities, shipboard diversions, or sexy dominatrices. But these women were real pirates who led lives just as adventurous and colorful as the male counterparts. They captured ships, planned attacks, and led fleets just as men did, in some cases even better.

We know more about some of these women than about others. Most of their exploits are not well documented. Mary Read and Anne Bonny left a trial record, and Cheng I Sao's crimes were reported in the newspapers of her time. But for many of our pirates, we have to rely on local lore and handed-down gossip.

Many prowled the seas during the Golden Age of Piracy, between the sixteenth and eighteenth centuries—an era that saw a great deal of trade between Europe and the Americas. Shipping lines were well established and most pirates simply had to wait patiently for a ship to sail into their traps. Several accounts of capture and pillage remain from that era, and from these come many clues to our pirates' way of life. A section at the back of this book on the "Classic Pirate Lifestyle" includes short descriptions of what life was like for women on pirate ships during the Golden Age—the rules and regulations, punishments, victuals, fashion, and frigging. I've also included a short list of books for anyone interested in reading further about the adventures of these marauding women.

Arrrr.

—Sara Lorimer

1860s
New York State

Sadie the Goat

Sadie the Goat

In 1869, in lower Manhattan, amid blocks of seedy slums, pawnshops, rescue missions, and gambling dens, there lived a young woman known as Sadie the Goat. New York was the largest and wealthiest city in the country, but Sadie's was not a wealthy part of town. Tuberculosis and diarrhea were the leading causes of death. Ragpickers went door-to-door trading anything from old food to broken furniture. Horses dropped thousands of pounds of manure on the cobblestone streets every day, and nobody was responsible for cleaning it up. Lines of drying laundry hung out the windows. Garbage piled in mounds in the gutter, sometimes several feet high. Sadie's neighborhood, the Fourth Ward—the "Bloody Fourth," known for its frequent violence—was the site of the densest population crush anywhere in the world.

She spent much of her time with a street gang. Mugging people on the streets of the Fourth Ward, Sadie would headbutt her victims

in the stomach [hence the nickname] and then let her gang fleece the unfortunates of cash and goods. It was small change, but it was something to do.

Sadie was a regular on Water Street, the Fourth Ward's main drag and a favorite of sailors and those looking for underworld fun. A travel guide of the day called it the most violent street on the continent; another warned readers absolutely to steer clear after dark. The Fourth Ward Hotel kept a trapdoor to dump corpses into the East River. The street had no shortage of saloons and their unlicensed cousins, called "blind tigers," which served the locals, slumming gentry, and the criminals who preyed on all alike. On the corner of Water and Dover Streets was one of the roughest taverns of all, the Hole-in-the-Wall, the favorite basement hangout of Sadie the Goat.

By far the scariest bouncer at the Hole-in-the-Wall was Gallus Mag—a six-foot-plus Englishwoman with a truncheon tied to her wrist and a revolver tucked in her belt. Mag had a unique way of dealing with rowdy drunks: smacking the lout with her truncheon, dragging him to the door with his ear held firmly in her teeth and, if she was in the mood, biting off the ear before tossing its owner into the street. The ears were added to her collection, which she kept in a

pickling jar behind the bar. One spring night Sadie ran afoul of Mag, and the next ear in the pickling jar was Sadie's.

After this, Sadie decided it was time to take a sabbatical from the Hole-in-the-Wall. Tired of making chump change with her old gang, Sadie shifted her attention over to the docks on the West Side, looking to throw in with a more successful band of hoodlums. There were plenty to choose from: the Daybreak Boys, the Buckoos, the Hookers, the Swamp Angels, the Slaughter Housers, the Border Gang, the Patsy Conroys, the Short Tails. She joined the Charlton Street Gang, young men with names like "Flabby Brown," "Big Mike," and "Big Brew," who spent their days in an abandoned gin mill and their nights stealing goods from ships on the North River, raiding them from rowboats. Sadie helped row for miles, hidden under piers, with oars muffled by rags. Climbing onto their targeted ship by its anchor chains, the gang grabbed whatever they could from the ship's deck or hold and rowed back to fence their loot in New York's pawnshops.

River and harbor piracy offered a great opportunity in Sadie's time. Pirates made off with more valuables than any other thieves in the city, but the competition was fierce. In 1850 the New York City chief of police estimated that there were fifty gangs and between four and five hundred river pirates in the Fourth Ward, with additional pirates dropping by from New Jersey and Brooklyn. By 1858 the city had only begun to address the situation by organizing the first harbor police patrol: a handful of men in rowboats. The police had a coup two years later when they captured river pirate and murderer Albert W. Hicks. More than ten thousand people turned out to see Hicks hanged on Bedloe's Island, swarming the island in steamboats, oyster sloops, barges, yachts, and rowboats—a spectacular demonstration

of what the city thought of pirates, but not the sort of thing to give Sadie pause.

Sadie took her piracy seriously, and by force of personality became the leader of the gang. She read up on pirate traditions and incorporated hallmarks of pirate lore into her crew's methods. They held prisoners for ransom after she heard that pirates had once kidnapped Julius Caesar, and she made her victims—and any crew members who angered her—walk the plank, a trait of fictional, and not historical, pirates.

The old Charlton Street Gang had worked an area unusual for river pirates: Manhattan's west side, dismissed as fruitless by their pirate brethren. The vessels docked here were mostly ocean-bound steamers and sailing ships whose owners protected their investments with especially vigilant watchmen and extra lighting on the piers. Soon after Sadie joined the gang, she realized that they needed to cast their efforts farther afield to make any real money. Under her leadership the gang stole a high-quality sloop, raised a Jolly Roger, and rampaged north, raiding farms and riverside mansions along the banks of the Hudson River as far upstate as Albany. Their loot was likely still small-time—food, a few valuables, and some cash.

But Sadie's exciting life of piracy soon came to an end. Farmers in the Hudson Valley united against the gang; Sadie found her raids met with gunfire, and notoriety forced the crew to abandon their distinctive sloop. Police patrolling New York's harbor prevented them from returning to their old hunting grounds on the North River. Defeated, Sadie and her crew slunk back to their gin mill.

After hosting seven murders in two months, the Hole-in-the-Wall was closed down by the police. Marking the end of an era, Gallus Mag reached into her pickle jar before the bar's last call to fish out Sadie's ear and return it to her former enemy. Sadie wore her ear in a locket hanging around her neck for the rest of her days in the Fourth Ward.

1801-1810

South China Sea

Cheng I Sao

Cheng I Sao

The greatest pirate of all time by the numbers, Cheng I Sao [sometimes called "Madame Ching" or "Cheng"] controlled a fleet of two thousand junks and had more than eighty thousand pirates—men, women, and children—at her command. A brilliant military tactician, she organized raids from her headquarters in Macao, and her pirates ruled much of the South China Sea and passages of the Pearl River.

Cheng I Sao, born Hsi-kai, was raised in the Chinese countryside and worked as a prostitute in a Cantonese brothel. She was a great beauty, driving Chinese historians to flights of poetry ["Skin . . . the tint of rich cream . . . at the cheek a deep rose. Her eyes were black and would shine like jet . . ."]. One reports that men were so enchanted by her that they "grew confused." Her mouth was voluptuous, and her slinky figure reminded admirers of that of a dancing girl.

It was common practice for pirates to bring prostitutes aboard ship when anchored, and Hsi-kai's beauty caught the attention of a band of pirates sent ashore by their leader, the extremely powerful, incredibly ugly Cheng I, to fetch women for him. When Hsi-kai was presented to Cheng I he found her so beautiful—and brave—that he begged her to marry him. Her first reaction was to try to scratch his eyes out, but on further consideration, given the choice between prostitution and piracy, she chose the latter, agreeing to the marriage only on the condition that she share equally in her husband's power. Cheng wasn't going to say no, and after their wedding in 1801 Hsi-kai became known as Cheng I Sao, or the wife of Cheng I.

Cheng I Sao and her husband built their massive pirate fleet from the tens of thousands of men, women, and children driven by famine and hunger who sailed the busy shipping lanes of the South China Sea looking for ships to attack. The couple consolidated their power by uniting warring pirate gangs. In 1805, they organized a truce between the seven pirate leaders of Kwangtung Province, and drew up an agreement outlining how the pirates would do business, under which each ship was registered and all raids had to be authorized.

The couple's fleet attacked fishing boats, cargo ships, and junks; on land, they pillaged coastal villages, rice fields, orange groves, and markets. Even coastal military garrisons were not safe, as Cheng I Sao led her men in raids for provisions. They once brought the city of Macao to the brink of crisis, blockading the port until the city was down to a two-day supply of rice.

Their main business was selling "protection," which they forced on ships and people living on the coast. The pirates sold signed documents guaranteeing the buyer a year free from attack [shorter stretches were also available]. The certificates could be

bought directly from the pirates or from agents working for them on land, and not only did pirates actually keep their word, they also honored protection certificates of other pirate gangs. Particularly lucrative was their protection of the booming Cantonese salt trade; by 1805, almost every salt ship leaving Canton had bought protection from pirates.

Kidnapping was also lucrative. The pirates abducted individuals and even entire villages to be held in exchange for cash, cloth, opium, and other goods. Cheng I Sao was careful to sprinkle garlic water on her captives' faces, which was believed to protect them from gunfire—not out of humanitarian concern, but to protect her investment.

When the time came for fighting, Madame Cheng's pirates, known as the "wasps of the ocean," had a well-earned reputation for ferocity. Merchant crews who resisted were tortured horribly and left as a lesson to others, and navy sailors met gruesome deaths whether they resisted or not. Madame Cheng paid her crews cash for each head they brought back from their attacks on shore; raiders could be seen fighting with five or six bloody heads hanging over their shoulders, tied together by their hair. Heading into battle, she gave her crews a fiery concoction of wine and gunpowder to drink, to make them fierce, and after the fight was over her pirates were known to eat the hearts of their victims. Military officials were understandably terrified of them and would often sabotage their own ships in an attempt to avoid battles. If that didn't work and they were still ordered to attack, they might "accidentally" fire their guns while sneaking up on the pirates, giving the pirates a chance to escape.

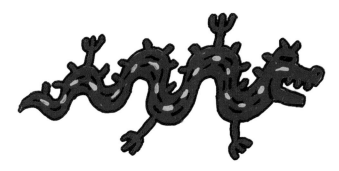

Cheng I died off the coast of Vietnam on 16 November, 1807, at the age of forty-two. There are various accounts of his death: blown overboard, captured and tortured, hit by a cannonball. All business, Madame Cheng donned a robe embroidered with gold, red, purple, and blue dragons and, carrying her late husband's favorite sword and wearing his war helmet, confronted the heads of the pirate council, demanding and getting sole leadership of the criminal confederation she and her husband had engineered.

But she needed help—a new lieutenant to command her largest fleet, an armada of three hundred junks and forty thousand pirates; someone unquestionably loyal but also well established in the pirate hierarchy. She chose Chang Pao, the twenty-one-year-old adopted son of Cheng I.

Chang Pao, who came from a family of fishermen, was abducted by the pirates as a teenager. Cheng I had had sexual relations with Chang Pao as part of the boy's initiation into the pirate gang, later adopting him and giving him command of a junk. Because Chang Pao had no other allegiances in the world of piracy, not having come from a pirate family, he was the perfect choice. Cheng I Sao sealed the deal by sleeping with him; the two married a few years later. Madame Cheng remained the commander in chief, leaving the day-to-day business to Chang Pao.

The armada was divided into six color-coded fleets, varying in number and size, from rowboats to oceangoing junks that held four hundred pirates, with clear chains of command in each fleet. Maintaining order was a complicated matter, and the couple drew up strict new laws governing the pirates' behavior. Any pirate who disobeyed a command or issued an unauthorized command lost his or her head. Also beheaded were pirates who stole from the common treasury, or who raped female captives. [Mutual consent was no excuse: the pirate was still beheaded and the woman was thrown overboard with a weight tied to her legs.] The first time a pirate went ashore without permission, his or her ears were split; if caught a second time, the penalty was death. Other crimes were rewarded with flogging, imprisonment in irons, or quartering.

Cheng I Sao herself took part in numerous raids, attacking her victims with dagger and cutlass. She prayed before every attack. Chang Pao built a temple on the deck of his largest ship; they also watched for omens, and a bad sign meant calling off a raid. A typical foray might begin with a small scouting boat with a few pirates pretending to be fishermen. They would chat up the crew of the target vessel [almost never European ships, which were considered more trouble than they were worth] and assess how difficult they might be to plunder. Once given the order to attack, the pirates converged on the vessel by sailing, rowing, swimming, and even running along shore. A fearsome sight; each pirate carried at least two swords—strapped under their arms if they had to swim—as they swarmed their prey.

When the fighting was over it was time to divide up the booty. One fifth of the goods went to the pirates who carried out the attack; the rest went into the common pool. Plunder ranged from the expected money and valuables to household items such as cloth,

quilts, nails, and firewood; stolen provisions included rice, fish, fresh water, vegetables, sugar, tea, and alcohol.

Female captives were divided up by quality. By Cheng I Sao's rules they were to be set free, but this order was frequently disobeyed. An informal system reserved pretty captives as wives or concubines for the male pirates; ugly captives were returned to shore, free of charge; and those in-between were held for ransom. Those whose ransom never reached the pirates, or who couldn't afford the cost, were auctioned off with the pretty ones on the ship. If a pirate bought a captive she was considered his wife, and he had to remain faithful to her—or face execution. Despite this wholesome oath, many women leapt overboard to drown rather than face marriage to one of their captors.

Government attempts to stop Cheng I Sao ranged from arresting her arms suppliers and trying to cut off her fleet's access to food and goods, to direct attacks on her ships. All met with failure. In 1808 alone, her pirates sank sixty-three imperial junks, and the navy was forced to hire thirty fishing boats in an effort to protect Canton. By 1809 Cheng I Sao was at the height of her power.

That September, Chinese authorities called for international help. The East India Company sent the *Mercury,* a ship with fifty men and twenty cannons, and Portugal leased the government six men-of-war. Cheng I Sao's junks were fast—but the arrival of heavily armed, steam-powered European gunboats meant trouble.

After a few months of this pressure, Cheng I Sao decided to give up the pirate life. Rivalries between her Red and Black Flag fleets were tearing apart her confederation; the new gunboats were a headache; and several of her most trusted men left her for the law-abiding life. On 18 April, 1810, Cheng I Sao and several of her female

pirates went to the governor-general's house in Canton to accept the government's offer of amnesty and negotiate the best deal possible for their surrender. Two days later, more than seventeen thousand of her pirates turned themselves in, handing in their weapons and 226 junks, but keeping their plunder. They were offered military jobs and some [including Cheng Pao, who kept a private fleet of junks and was given the rank of lieutenant] joined the navy they once fought so fiercely. Relatively few were punished: 60 were banished for two years, 151 exiled permanently, and 126 were executed.

Cheng I Sao and Chang Pao retired first to Canton, then later settled in Fukien. In 1813 she gave birth to a son, Cheng Yü-lin. In 1822 Chang Pao, by now a colonel, died of natural causes at age thirty-six. Twice widowed and not yet fifty years old, Cheng I Sao moved back to Canton, opened a gambling house, and rumor has it, embarked on a secondary career as a smuggler. She died peacefully at age sixty-nine.

9th century A.D.

Baltic and North Seas

Alfhild

NORTH SEA

STOCKHOLM

HELSINKI

BALTIC SEA

COPENHAGEN

Alfhild

In the ninth century the waters of the north seas were bristling with Viking longboats full of scruffy Scandinavian warriors who terrorized ships and even cities along the coasts of Europe. Siward, the Scandinavian king of the Goth tribe, had a daughter, Alfhild, who according to legend was so breathtakingly beautiful that from an early age she kept her face hidden lest she stir the passions of men. Even so, her beauty was known throughout the empire. Wary of suitors, the king kept Alfhild housebound, and gave her a pair of vipers for pets to further discourage male attention. To keep things interesting, though, he also decreed that if any man could make his way past the snakes unscathed, he would allow the suitor to take Alfhild's hand in marriage. If the suitor failed he would be beheaded [whether or not he survived the vipers' bites] and his head impaled on a stake, left as a warning to others.

This challenge proved irresistible to a young man named Alf, the son of the Danish king Sygarus. Wrapped in a bloody animal hide, Alf advanced on the vipers with a spear and a pair of tongs, which clasped a lump of red-hot iron. As the first viper bared its fangs to attack, Alf dispatched it by thrusting the burning metal into its mouth. When the second viper slithered to protect its mistress, Alf killed it with his expertly thrown spear. Alfhild should have been his, but old King Siward changed the rules: his daughter would have the right to refuse any suitor, even one who'd made it this far. Alfhild was willing to give the brave, good-looking Dane a chance, but her mother warned her sternly: *Are good looks enough for you to give up your chastity? Shouldn't you judge his virtue, not just his appearance?* Disturbed by her mother's advice, Alfhild turned a cold eye on young Alf. She slipped out of the wedding plans, donned men's clothes, and ran off—to assume the life of a roving raider.

In the course of battle, Alfhild met and joined forces with like-minded women out for adventure, including one named Groa, who would become her attendant and right-hand girl. The women formed a bandit gang; early in its career they came upon a band of mariner thieves who were mourning the death of their leader. One account has Alfhild being elected the new captain by the pirates' acclaim for her incredible beauty. Perhaps. She may also have simply seized their vessel. Certainly her daring leadership soon impressed the pirates, who attacked and robbed ships for several months in the icy waters of the Atlantic, before long amassing a fleet of ships. Unfortunately, the details of their raids are not recorded, only that Alfhild led them bravely, beyond what was expected of a woman's courage.

Meanwhile, Alf wasn't ready to give up. His heart broken, his pride wounded, he was determined to claim his prize. Joining the

Danish expeditions sent to stop Alfhild's pirate fun, he caught up to her fleet as it rested in a Finnish harbor. When she saw strange ships—Alf's ships—approaching, she decided that aggression was the best defense and, still disguised as a man, ordered her pirates to launch an attack. Alf's men hesitated, as they were outnumbered, but Alf, worried about his reputation, threw himself into battle, leading his men onto Alfhild's ship and running from bow to stern, slaughtering any of Alfhild's crew that tried to stop him. In the frenzy, Borgar, Alf's right-hand man, knocked off Alfhild's helmet, revealing her face to her spurned suitor.

It is unclear if Alfhild was pleased to see Alf or whether the pleasure was all his. In any case, the pair were married, Alfhild went back to wearing women's clothes, and she bore Alf a daughter, Gurid. Borgar married Alfhild's shipmate, Groa, and they had a son, Harald. Here Alfhild drops from the history books, but the stories of her adventures have entertained Scandinavian children ever since.

late 18th century
New England Coast

Rachel Wall

PORTLAND

ISLE OF SHOALS

BOSTON

ATLANTIC OCEAN

Rachel Wall

Pirate Rachel Wall was the last woman to be hanged in the state of Massachusetts, in 1789. Up to then, her career was an unqualified success: raiding ships for two years up and down the coast of New England, she and her crew stole thousands of dollars worth of cash and goods from the local shipping trade. When the law finally caught up with her it wasn't for piracy, although she confessed her pirate ways before the hanging; it was for highway robbery.

Born in 1760 in Carlisle, Pennsylvania, to a large family of farmers, Rachel's pirate life was an escape from her upright background. Her parents were devout Presbyterians—her father led the family in prayer twice a day—and as she grew up she found their piety stifling. While a teenager she twice ran away from home. The first

time she seems to have come back on her own; the second time she eloped with Boston fisherman and former Revolutionary War privateer George Wall. The couple hit the road, first to Philadelphia, then to New York City for three months, then to Boston. George left Rachel in Boston abruptly, as though she were a stranger, but at least she was out of Carlisle. She took a job as a servant on Beacon Hill and was content. Rumors that George had gone to Canada to privateer [to sail with a private ship licensed by the government to attack enemy ships] were confirmed when he came back a few months later, pockets full of plunder, to lure her [her confession claimed] into the pirate life.

After a weekend of boozing, the couple discovered that the schooner George and five of his pals were supposed to be working on had gone to sea without them. The gang borrowed, and never returned, a sloop from a harbor in Essex, and decided to work the area of the Isles of Shoals, a group of small islands off the coast of Maine rumored to have once been a hideout for Blackbeard. George still fished occasionally—the crew pretended to be a family of fishermen—but their real aim was plunder.

Their modus operandi was particularly crafty. They anchored in the islands with a heavy mooring when storms hit and, after the turbulence passed, they flew a distress flag and set the ship adrift, having set it up to seem to be damaged and in danger of foundering. Rachel stood on deck and screamed for help. When other ships responded, Rachel's cronies would murder the Good Samaritans for their trouble, steal everything of value on the rescue vessel, and then sink it as though it had been a victim of the storm.

Their first target was a fishing schooner from Plymouth. The pirates killed the four men aboard and threw their bodies over the

side, then stole $360 and the ship's fittings. Their next victims were the seven-man crew of a Penobscot River sloop, which they took for $550 in cash and $870 worth of goods. Rachel and the gang lured the ship's captain and mate, then two more sailors, to their ship to help "patch a leak," killing them and then the remaining three sailors when they seized their vessel. Through the two summers of Rachel's pirate career, 1781 and 1782, the Walls took at least twelve vessels, killing twenty-four men and stealing $6,000 in cash and an unknown amount of goods that they generally sold in Boston and Portsmouth, often claiming to have found them washed up on the beach after the most recent storm.

In September of 1782 the pirate sloop was battered by a hurricane. A giant wave swept George and another crewmember overboard, and when the mast snapped, Rachel and the others raised their

distress flag in earnest this time, letting themselves be rescued by a brig from New York without killing its crew.

Chastened by the ordeal, Rachel made her way back to Boston, found work as a maid, and tried to resume the morally upright life her parents had always wanted for her. It didn't take. One spring night in 1787, according to her confession, Rachel crept onto a ship tied up at Boston's Long Wharf. In the unlocked cabin where the captain and the mate were sleeping, she ran her hand under the captain's bed and came up with quite a haul—more than thirty pounds of gold, crowns, and small change—and skulked back off the ship. She admitted later that she burned through the money quickly, "in company as lewd and wicked" as herself.

It was too easy not to do again. Soon afterward, Rachel broke into a sloop at Doane's Wharf, in Boston. Again a sleeping captain, and the crew equally unaware in their berths in steerage. This time she scored a silver watch, which caught her eye as it hung above the captain's head, as well as a handful of change and the silver buckles off the captain's shoes. Pocketing her shiny prizes, she crept away to spend the booty with her shifty friends.

One evening in September 1789 a Miss Bender was robbed on a Boston street, and a witness accused Rachel of the crime. Although she pleaded her innocence to the end, she was found guilty and

sentenced to hang. In a jailhouse confession on 8 October 1789, the night before her death, she admitted to the ship robberies but was vague about what she, George, and the crew had done in their glory days of plundering ships together. She said she forgave her husband for introducing her to the pirate life, and that she hoped her death would be a warning to young women everywhere to stay away from wicked company.

1710s–1720

The Caribbean

Mary Read *and*

Anne Bonny

MIAMI

HAVANA

CUBA

CARIBBEAN SEA

KINGSTON

Mary Read and Anne Bonny

Mary Read was disguised as a boy the moment she was born. Her mother, married to a sailor, gave birth to her first child, their son, while her husband was at sea. The sailor's mother—their chief means of support—contributed one crown a week, about enough for five loaves of bread and a few pots of ale. The sailor was still at sea when Mary's mother realized, to her dismay, that she was pregnant again. Desperate, she fled with her son to a rural area outside London, hiding the pregnancy from her mother-in-law and still collecting their allowance. The boy died soon after, however, and it seemed now Mary's mother had a way out. Telling no one and furtively disposing of the body, she would try to pass the new, illegitimate child off as the dead son. When she gave birth to a daughter, Mary, she went ahead with the plan, dressing Mary in boys' clothes and raising the girl as she would a son. Her husband never returned to discover the deception, and Mary's grandmother died

when Mary was thirteen, never realizing that Mary was a girl. But when the grandmother left nothing of her estate to her "only grandson," Mary, still in disguise, was sent to work as a footboy for a Frenchwoman in London.

A few years of this was enough for Mary, and she found relief by enlisting on a royal man-of-war as a "powder monkey," hauling gunpowder to the sailors working cannons. Soon bored of this, too, she deserted and made her way to Flanders, where she signed on with the Flemish army, joined a regiment, and practiced her dueling skills.

Mary's tent mate turned out to be a handsome Flemish soldier and, after a few months of bunking with him, Mary was clearly in love. She longed to reveal herself as a woman, but at what price? She volunteered for dangerous missions to be near him and made attempts to get him to think of her . . . differently. One night she managed the courage to let him discover her sex, to his surprise and delight. They should take advantage of the shared tent right away, he suggested, but Mary rebuffed him, holding out for a wedding ring. Soon after, Mary marched into town to buy her first piece of women's clothing—a wedding dress.

Of course the marriage meant Mary and her husband were forced to leave the army. Charmed by the couple, and by Mary's impressive service as an officer, her fellow soldiers gave Mary a small amount of money to set up house. The newlyweds settled near the Castle of Breda in the Netherlands, close to their former garrison, and opened a small inn, the Three Horses. Most of their customers were soldiers, and business was good until peace came, the soldiers left, and the inn went bankrupt. Mary's husband died soon after, and creditors were circling. In women's clothing Mary had only a woman's options, so she put on her trousers and went to find work,

once more as a soldier and then as a sailor on a Dutch merchant-ship sailing for the West Indies. When the ship was attacked by English pirates in the Caribbean and the pirates discovered the presence of a fellow Englishman on the ship, they gave him a choice: join us or die. Signing the pirate ship's articles as Sailor Read, Mary officially turned pirate.

*A*nne Bonny was also born into duplicitous circumstance. Her father, a lawyer, lived with his wife in a town near Cork, Ireland; Anne's mother was his maid. The scandal of Anne's birth split the family apart, and her father moved with the maid and his new daughter to the American colonies, probably to Charleston. Here Anne's father found success in business and Anne grew up in luxury. Stories of her childhood and youth—that she killed a servant with a knife and beat an overamorous suitor within an inch of his life—suggest young Anne had quite a temper. When she was about sixteen years old, she fell for the charms of James Bonny, a small-time pirate. They eloped, and her father, furious, disinherited her. This was inconvenient for Bonny, who'd married Anne for her money. Looking for easy times, James and Anne Bonny moved to the island of New Providence, the center of the Bahamas and home to some two thousand pirates. What they got up to here isn't clear, but it was probably at least a little shady [James may at one point have tried to "sell" Anne in a local tavern]. Anne spent a lot of time hanging out on the waterfront without him, sometimes dressed as a man, sometimes not. Here, the not-yet-twenty-year-old Anne met and ran away with the flashy pirate John Rackham to begin her own life of adventure on the high seas.

*J*ohn Rackham—a ladies' man and a snappy dresser—was known as "Calico Jack" for his distinctive striped pants. He and his crew had been raiding ships and generally enjoying themselves in the Caribbean for a while before he met Anne. By 1717 piracy in the Caribbean was so rampant that the shipping trade was at a crawl, and a desperate King George I of England issued a proclamation pardoning all pirates in the West Indies if only they would please stop their plundering. Mary Read and her English pirate shipmates, working the same waters as Jack's crew, took the king up on his offer and left their ship to settle on shore, probably in the Bahamas. Whatever enterprise the reformed thieves found for themselves there failed, and they soon ran out of money. In 1718 the Governor of the Bahamas began fitting out privateers—pirates enlisted for national duty to attack enemy vessels—to fight the Spaniards, and the following year Mary and others from her crew signed on to sail with one of the ships. Jack, too, had taken up first the king and then the governor on their offers: he and Mary were on the same ship. No sooner had the ship reached the open sea than the crew, led by Calico Jack, mutinied. Mary, still in men's clothes as "Sailor Read," joined the rebellion and once more chose the pirate life.

Among the ship's crew abducted in the mutiny was a young Englishman who caught Mary's eye and, once again, she started looking for a way to let it slip that she was a woman. She started spending more time with the Englishman, professing a dislike for piracy. Having been forced into larceny, he doubtless was pleased to find someone with whom to confide. Once Mary felt sure that he was sympathetic to her, she "accidentally" showed him her breasts. The Englishman demanded the truth—was she a woman? Yes, said Mary. They had been friends as men; could they be more?

Maybe so, but not for long. The Englishman had somehow offended another of the pirates while they were at anchor near a small island and the offense led to their scheduling a duel on shore the next day. Mary was anguished. She knew that the other pirate was a better fighter, and her Englishman would almost certainly be killed. Finding the offended pirate, Mary contrived an altercation and herself demanded a duel, scheduled two hours before the Englishman's. The next morning, Mary and the pirate met on the island armed with swords and pistols. Wielding her cutlass and gun with the skill of her soldiering days, she slashed the pirate while suffering not a scratch herself. For the love of one pirate, Mary killed another. Triumphant, Mary rushed back to tell the Englishman how she had [indirectly] saved his life. If he had liked her for her conversation, and lusted after her once he knew she was a woman, her dueling brought him to love. They swore their love for each other then and there, and Mary considered this just as good as a church wedding. They stayed together in secret on Jack's ship for a time before it returned to New Providence, where Jack met Anne. It wouldn't be long before they sailed together again on the same ship.

*C*alico Jack impressed Anne with his good looks, wealthy generosity, and pirate swagger. In their courtship, he vowed to give her an unspecified amount of money before they started living together, as recorded in a document they planned to give to Anne's husband, an

announcement of sorts that she wouldn't be coming back. When they asked a man named Richard Turnley to witness the signing, he refused and instead reported the adulterous couple to the governor, who threatened to have Anne imprisoned and whipped for her unladylike behavior. Knowing they couldn't freely be together on land, Anne and Calico Jack decided to run away. In a scheme they devised together, Anne scouted out a sloop to steal and one rainy midnight, in a stolen rowboat with eight pirate cohorts, they boarded the poorly guarded ship. Anne made straight for the cabin where the crew slept. The men woke to the sight of Anne holding a gun in one hand and a sword in the other. If they resisted, she hissed, she would blow their brains out. Meanwhile, the rest of the pirates managed to loose the ship's cables and take the sloop out to sea. The ship's crew, declining the offer to join the pirates, were sent packing in the stolen rowboat.

Dressed in men's clothes [but not pretending to be a man] Anne went with Calico Jack on his voyages and attacks, fighting alongside him. At one point, when pregnancy interfered with her seafaring life, Anne went ashore to Cuba to stay with friends until giving birth, then left the child to return to her ship. Once more at sea, Anne's loyalty to Calico Jack was tested when she took a liking to a handsome young man on board. Unfortunately for Anne, the one she had her eye on was "Sailor Read," in trousers and sailing with her Englishman on Jack's ship. Mary at first deflected Anne's advances, angering a woman who was used to getting what she wanted, and finally had no choice but to reveal that she, too, was a woman.

The ridiculousness of the situation—not one but two women on a pirate ship—must have been a delight for them, and Mary and Anne quickly became friends. When Calico Jack saw that Anne had a

new favorite in the crew, he was furious until he was let in on the secret as well. The rest of the crew, with the exception of Mary's Englishman, continued to believe Mary was a man.

In August of 1720, Mary, Anne, Calico Jack, and the rest of their crew sailed their new stolen sloop, the *William*, along the north and west coasts of Jamaica, attacking small fishing boats, usually making off with little more than the fishermen's nets and tackle. In early September they made seven or eight such raids off Harbour Island in the Bahamas. Despite the minor nature of their plundering, Jack and the gang drew the ire of the authorities, who issued a proclamation declaring Calico Jack Rackham and his crew "Enemies to the Crown of Great Britain." The governor had ordered Anne to return to her husband, and this was how she had obeyed his orders? In November, off the coast of Negril on the west end of Jamaica, a sloop captain named Bonnevie saw the *William* fire a cannon near the shore, which seemed suspicious, and a Captain Barnet—commissioned to catch pirates—set after the ship in his own sloop. When the pirates refused to lower their sails and fired on Barnet, he returned the fire and brought down the *William*'s boom, effectively crippling the ship. The pirates—Mary Read, Anne Bonny, Calico Jack, and their crew of ten—after uneven resistance, surrendered. Barnet landed at Davis Cove, Jamaica, and turned over his captives to the militia, who kept them in jail in Spanish Town until their trial.

*A*nne and Mary stood trial two and a half months after their capture. Their shipmates had, twelve days earlier before the same judges, been found guilty and hanged. Anne had been permitted to visit Calico Jack in his cell the day of his execution. But instead of a

tearful farewell, she took the opportunity to curse Jack. Only Mary, Anne, and one other pirate had attempted to fight off Barnet's men—their shipmates remained drinking belowdecks. If Calico Jack "had fought like a Man" that night, Anne spat at him in his cell, he "need not have been hang'd like a Dog." Faced with the same court, the same charges, additional witnesses, and no legal representation, matters weren't looking good for Anne or Mary.

The charges included that they had made a wicked agreement with the other [now dead] pirates to "rob, plunder, and take, all such Persons . . . which they should meet with on the high Sea"; that they had attacked seven fishing boats and put the fishermen "in Corporal Fear of their Lives," but let them go unharmed after stealing their tackle; that they had attacked two more merchant sloops, a schooner, and another sloop in similar fashion. Here the court registrar paused in his litany of charges to ask for their pleas. *Not guilty,* Mary and Anne replied. The charges continued. A woman testified that the pirates had attacked her canoe. The captains of the victim ships and other witnesses came forward, testifying to Anne and Mary's role in the attacks: that they'd brandished swords and pistols, that they'd threatened harm, that "they were both very profligate, cursing and swearing much, and very ready and willing to do any Thing on Board." The judge turned to Anne and Mary. "Do you have any defense to make? Any witness to be sworn on your behalf, or would you like to cross-examine the witnesses just heard from?" *No,* they replied. While the court commissioners withdrew to consider the evidence, a guard led Anne and Mary back to their cells.

The ruling was as expected. Found guilty, the women were asked once again if they had anything to say. They did not. "You Mary Read and Anne Bonny, alias Bonn, are to go from hence to the place

whence you came, and from thence to the place of execution; where you shall be severally hanged by the neck, until you are severally dead. And God of His infinite mercy be merciful to both your souls." The death sentence, the expected punishment for piracy, was handed down to about forty pirates a year; but Anne and Mary had a plan.

My Lord! they cried out. *We plead our bellies!*

The pirates were pregnant.

After the excitement in the courtroom died down, the judge ordered the women back to their cells. The trial adjourned until an examination could be made to determine the truth of their claim. A pregnant woman would not hang, Mary and Anne knew; even if this was only a postponement of their death sentences, it was something.

Mary Read—servant, soldier, wife, innkeeper, sailor, duelist, pirate—died a mundane death of a fever while in prison. On 28 April, 1721, her body was buried in the parish of St. Catherine in Jamaica. As for Anne Bonny, she was never hanged, and there's no reliable record of either her death or her release from prison. She simply disappeared.

mid-17th century

Mediterranean Sea,
Atlantic Ocean

Charlotte de Berry

ATLANTIC OCEAN

LONDON ★

★ PARIS

★ MADRID

MEDITERRANEAN SEA

AFRICA

Charlotte de Berry

As a young woman, Charlotte de Berry was drawn to the seedier side of life, sneaking out at night from the strictures of her staid English upbringing to hang out on the docks. Here, amid the drinking, thieving, and gambling, blending in with the riffraff, and disguised as a man, Charlotte could be free.

One fateful night she crossed paths with a thirty-year-old sailor in the royal navy named Jack Jib [né Jack Melees], who at first thought Charlotte a boy. Smitten, Charlotte set him straight by revealing herself to him in a moment when they were alone. Sparks flew, and Jack married Charlotte soon after.

After just a month of wedded bliss, Jack was called to return to the navy. Not wanting to be left out of the action, Charlotte enlisted and served on the same ship, pretending to be her husband's brother, "Dick." The "brothers" were inseparable, fighting side by side in six major sea battles. It was a perfect arrangement, until the

ship's second mate, the scheming Lieutenant House, discovered Charlotte's secret. Rather than turning her in, which would have led to her being kicked off the ship and out of his reach, he decided to get rid of Jack instead. As lieutenant, he arranged for Jack to serve the most dangerous duties on deck while in battle, hoping nature might take its course. But the plan backfired: not only did Jack survive, but "Dick" fought fiercely beside him, the secret sweethearts growing closer still in the heat of combat. Switching tactics, House accused Jack of mutiny. The trial came down to the lieutenant's word against Jack's. Jack was found guilty and sentenced to be flogged by the entire fleet, a severe sentence for a severe crime. As he was rowed in a dinghy from ship to ship, an officer from each vessel gave him a dozen lashes with a cat-o'-nine-tails. The punishment killed him.

To House's mind, now that Jack was out of the way, Charlotte was his, but she wanted none of it. After stabbing him with her trusty dagger, she jumped ship while anchored at an English port. On the run and now dressed again as a woman, Charlotte made her way to London, where she worked as an "entertainer" [details are scarce] in the city's waterfront cafés.

The café scene didn't attract the best sort, and one admirer, Captain Wilmington of the Guinea merchantman *Normandy,* kidnapped Charlotte and had her taken aboard his ship, bound for Africa. Once they were under way, Wilmington—cruel, portly, and middle-aged—forced Charlotte to marry him. The crew wasn't fond of the captain either; Charlotte soon managed to lead them in a mutiny against the captain, her husband, killing him. The crew, now outlaws facing hanging for mutiny, threw caution to the wind. They renamed their ship the *Trader* [despite a superstition that renaming a ship brings bad luck] and decided to be pirates, with Charlotte,

again dressed in men's clothing and adopting the *nom de guerre* "Captain Rudolph," as their leader.

Charlotte stepped into her new role with relish, prowling the Atlantic coast from England to Spain and the Mediterranean Sea, and stories of her ferocity and cruelty, including once having a captive's mouth sewn shut, spread quickly.

Storm and battle damage forced Charlotte to dock the *Trader* in Granada, Spain, for repairs. While ashore, she resumed her female identity, catching the eye of José Sandano, the son of a wealthy planter. He fell in love with Charlotte, joined her crew, gave her his fortune, and married her in short order. At sea, the *Trader* met a terrible storm and sank, leaving only eight survivors, including Charlotte and José, clinging to a makeshift raft. After eight days with neither food nor water, the survivors came to a chilling agreement: to draw lots, with the loser to be killed and eaten by the others.

José drew the short straw, whereupon the first mate shot him dead. Horribly, a merchant ship appeared on the horizon just moments later and Charlotte's crew was rescued—all except for poor José. The remaining seven pretended to be traders whose vessel had sunk in the storm. Charlotte's luck took yet another turn for the worse when, just days after their rescue, the ship that had saved her crew was itself attacked by pirates. As "Captain Rudolph," Charlotte fought off the raiders and saved the ship's crew—but her triumph meant nothing to her. With a cry of "José!" Charlotte de Berry leapt overboard to drown.

1920s-1930s

Pearl River, China

Lai Choi San

CANTON

PEARL RIVER

MACAO

HONG KONG

SOUTH CHINA SEA

Lai Choi San

Chinese pirate Lai Choi San raided ships as recently as the 1930s, piloting her brown-sailed junk with wily, predatory skill in the waters around the Portuguese colony of Macao. In her thirties, she commanded twelve fully armored oceangoing junks—seven she had inherited from her father, and five she'd picked up herself under less than legal circumstances. From her lookout perch, an empty packing crate on the top deck of her flagship's two-story poop, with two female attendants always at her side, she led her crew on brutal raids and amassed a fortune so enormous that she was known by some as the "Mountain of Wealth," but also by the more regal nickname "Queen of the Macao Pirates."

Lai Choi San had a reputation for seriousness as well as cruelty. It's said she never laughed, and that the toughness of her expression was matched by the intelligence in her eyes. On land, where she

owned gambling houses, the short and slender pirate was the picture of femininity and refinement: white satin robes with jade buttons, green silk slippers, jade pins holding her jet black hair in a knot on her neck, and gold rings on her left hand. At sea, though, she was all business, kicking off the slippers and swapping the robes for sturdy pants and a loose-fitting black blouse. She went barefoot, and kept her ever-alert eyes shaded with a wide-brimmed straw hat.

She was the only girl in her family. Her four brothers all died young; as a frail child she was not expected to survive. Her father, who was the inspector of Macao's enormous fishing fleet, took her on his rounds and instilled in her an appreciation for hard work as well as easy money—he had started work as a coolie and then found his way into the good life as an official able to use his position to extort money and foster his secondary career as a pirate. After he died in a fight with a rival pirate gang, she stepped into his shoes as both official and criminal. As "inspector," Lai Choi San made rounds of the fishing fleets and defended them from pirates, sinking pirate ships and capturing their crews or merely chasing them away. As the Pirate Queen, she extorted tributes—cash and goods—from the captains of fishing ships in her waters under threat of murder. In neither capac-

ity was she very popular with the hundreds of other pirate gangs who worked the South China Sea, with whom she was constantly at war. By necessity, her junks were the best and fastest she could find.

When she spotted a vessel ripe for plunder, she commanded her pirate crew to race toward it. As they drew close to the target, her men donned cartridge belts and grabbed their pistols and rifles from a cabin next to her quarters. When they were within hailing distance, one of the pirates would fire a few warning shots, and this was usually enough to make the ship lower its mainsail and surrender. If that didn't work, she would fire her cannons, filling the air with the smell of burnt black powder and the guns' shattering roar. After hasty and shouted negotiations, the captain of the captured ship rowed across to her junk in a dinghy, then went to the captain's quarters below deck to bargain as Lai Choi San kept an eye on things above deck, aloof.

She never spoke to her crew, a muscular lot, mostly men, who wore red kerchiefs and wide-brimmed hats or pith helmets to protect themselves from the tropical sun. Only the captain rated her attention, and that was only to give orders; his questions met with the curt impatience of someone who knows what she wants. Her female attendants, too, dealt only with the captain, who could best be described as obedient. She didn't bother to sail on patrols, spending this time in her finery at home or in her gambling houses on land, but she resolutely commanded all of her pirates' raids herself.

On one such raid, to collect payment from two delinquent fishing captains, she outlined her extortion process to a Finnish journalist whom she allowed on board her ship. As the captains lay bound hand and foot on the deck, Lai Choi San explained that simply killing them would mean paperwork, as well as dealing with their families. Instead, she would leave them on deck for a few days,

in the sun, without food, at the mercy of swarms of mosquitoes at night. Their families would pay the ransom, and if they didn't, she might send them a fingertip, an ear, or a bit of a nose to hurry things along. If that didn't work, she'd kill them. That was the custom, she explained, and everyone knew how it worked.

Lai Choi San owned a stately house in Macao and another well-appointed home in her village on the West River, but life on her junk was far less comfortable. Her cabin was too small to stand upright in—even squatting left little headroom—but what it lacked in size, she made up in lavish decoration. The walls were lined with brightly colored hardwood carvings; an image of the goddess A Ma, patroness of seafarers; and an ancestral tablet inscribed with her father's name. She burned incense nightly at various points on the ship as an offering to the gods of luck and in front of her father's tablet. She also enlisted Taoist priests to light fireworks on the dock as she began each new adventure, to ward off evil spirits.

Despite the pressures of running a successful business, Lai Choi San found the time to get married twice. Her first husband seems to have died suddenly after the couple had a quarrel. The second, she said, didn't really count as a "husband." She was said to have many lovers. She was the mother of two boys; her eldest son, she told the Finnish journalist, was going to school in Shanghai, and she had dreams for him to become a rice merchant and marry the rich girl he'd been engaged to since childhood. She'd heard about the "skyscrapers" in America, and wanted him to sail to the United States and buy one. She was grooming her younger son to be a pirate. To toughen him up, she sent him away to train on one of her junks, and though he was only five years old, she said, he was already smoking like a real man.

Lai Choi San's ultimate fate is a mystery, although the most popular versions have her either being blown up by a Japanese torpedo or captured by the authorities and imprisoned for life, only to escape and subsequently disappear. It's thought that Lai Choi San may have been the model for the villainous "Dragon Lady" character in Milton Caniff's popular newspaper comic strip of the 1930s and 1940s, "Terry and the Pirates."

1580s

Cornish Coast

Lady

Mary Killigrew

ATLANTIC OCEAN

LONDON

CORNWALL

Lady Mary Killigrew

Some choose piracy, others are forced, but Lady Mary Killigrew was born into it. In sixteenth-century England and Ireland it was not uncommon for the rich and royal to subsidize or strike out for themselves on "gentlemanly" pirate activities, an arrangement made easier by their status and wink-nudge relationships with port officers. Mary's father, Philip Wolverston, was known as the "Gentleman Pirate of Suffolk." Her brother Peter raided ships on the Irish seas; her cousins John Mitchell and John Penrose were known to dabble in the family trade as well. Mary had no objections to the family hobby, and married a pirate herself. Her husband, Sir John Killigrew, built an expensive house at Arwennack, near Pendennis Castle on the rugged and remote Cornish coast. The house ultimately proved a convenient warehouse for their plundered booty, as Sir John moved from investing in pirate enterprises to

leading the attacks himself. Lady Mary, not one to be left out of the action, followed suit, masterminding more than a few of their raids.

Damaged by a fierce storm one night in January 1582, the Spanish ship *Marie de San Sebastian* limped into Falmouth Harbor, spitting distance from Pendennis Castle, the Killigrew's favorite staging area for attacks. Lady Killigrew commanded a boarding party, seven Flemish sailors and two of her household servants—John Hawkins and Henry Kendall—in a raid on the ship. No discerning pillager, she demanded her motley crew seize every possible item of value. She came away with several rolls of Holland cloth, a welcomed bit of plunder, which she distributed to her family, and a small amount of money. She also managed a set of six leather chairs, but the guilt of her thievery—or perhaps the murder of the entire Spanish crew—tainted her spoils, and she ordered them taken from her sight and buried in the family garden.

Juan de Chavis and Captain Philip de Oryo, owners of the ill-fated Spanish vessel, caught word of who was responsible for the attack on their ship. They registered a complaint with the Cornwall Commission for Piracy, a lucky stroke for Mary. The corrupt commission, under the leadership of its president, Mary's son John, declared the attack to have been carried out by persons unknown. Unluckily for Mary, de Chavis and de Oryo then took their complaint to their friend the Earl of Bedford in London.

The Earl was a member of Queen Elizabeth's Privy Council, which meant he could bring the Spaniards' complaint directly to her. The queen had wanted to break the pirate ring in Falmouth Harbor for quite some time; deciding this was her golden opportunity, she appointed two of her men to look into the matter. They held hearings and called witnesses, including Lady Mary's granddaughter.

Mary's influential friends saved her from prosecution, but Hawkins and Kendall were hanged for crimes she had commanded.

After lying low for a few years, Lady Mary decided to try again. Acting on a tip, she had her pirates raid a German ship that she suspected held a cargo of pieces of eight, killing two of the crew-members. The local authorities, long willing to turn a blind eye to the activities of Cornwall's finest family, reached the end of their patience, and Mary was arrested. Fortunately, her son John had sufficient loot from his own pirate activities to pay bribes, and when Mary came to court she was acquitted. Although it's uncertain whether Lady Killigrew finally took this as a sign to retire, her son continued his plundering ways into the 1600s.

1550–1603

West Coast of Ireland

Grace O'Malley
(Granuaile)

Grace O'Malley (Granuaile)

Grace O'Malley plundered her first ship as a teenager and kept on raiding into her seventies—one of the longest pirate careers the seas have ever seen. Also known as Granuaile, Grace commanded respect and fear, a powerful woman in an age of powerful men. One legend has her burying more than nine tons of treasure, still undiscovered and presumably still guarded by her curse.

Born in Connaught on the west coast of Ireland, Grace grew up in her father's house, the stone fortress of Belcare, a damp, dark place enlivened by the occasional visits of mummers and musicians. Her clan's income came from piracy and fishing, and had for generations. Other O'Malley activities included deerhunting, gambling [of which Grace was famously fond], and fighting with the neighbors. Their motto: *Terra marique potens* [powerful by land and by sea]. When she was a girl, her father, Owen "Dubhdara" [Black Oak] O'Malley,

taught her how to sail, a traditionally male skill that served her well in her piracy career. At that time, the sea and rivers were the easiest means of travel and moving goods in Ireland, and the O'Malleys charged tolls for ships passing through their territory.

When she was sixteen or so, Grace married Dónal O'Flaherty, the son of a neighboring chieftain. Bringing a large dowry of household goods and livestock, she moved to his coastal castle at Bunowen. His family, which ruled the area around what is now Connemara under the motto "fortune favors the bold," had gotten along more or less peacefully with the O'Malleys for decades, but they often fought with other neighbors. Dónal was known as Dónal-an-Chogaidh [Dónal of the Battles]; some of his enemies called him An Cullagh, the cock, for his pride, which made his castle Cock's Castle.

While Dónal was occupied with his small but constant battles, Grace turned to providing "protection" to ships in the waters near their castle, as well as robbing ships outright. Grace and her men lay in wait in the uncharted inlets or behind coastal islands around Bunowen, striking out after merchant ships and barques with lightning speed. After taking what she wanted from the cargo she generally let the ships continue on to Galway.

When not busy plundering, Grace found time to raise a family. She and Dónal had a daughter, Margaret, and two sons, Owen and Murrough. Sometime around 1564, when Grace was in her mid-thirties, one of Dónal's fights left her a widow. The Joyce clan—Dónal's traditional enemies, who were more than likely responsible for his death—immediately attacked Cock's Castle. Grace repulsed the attack so soundly that the castle was popularly renamed Caisleán-an-Circa, or Hen's Castle, as it's still known to this day.

In a later battle, English forces tried to seize the castle by blockading Grace and a few of her men inside, cutting off all food and supplies. Determined to keep her home, she ordered the castle's metal roof to be torn down, melted in giant pots, and poured on the heads of the English soldiers from the parapets. Still besieged, she had one of her best men sneak out in the night to light a signal beacon, summoning aid and saving Hen's Castle.

According to custom, only men were allowed to become chieftain, and so despite Grace's bravery and leadership, Dónal's cousin was elected to succeed him; Grace and her sons inherited only a portion of Dónal's land [although Murrough would later win most of it back]. She returned to her father's lands and, against convention, many of Dónal's men loyally followed her. After her father died, most of his fleet came under her control, and although she could not be elected chieftain of the clan, she acted and was treated as one, or else there was hell to pay.

Returning from a foray, Grace docked at Howth, a port near Dublin, and went ashore in search of water and supplies for the last leg of her trip home. As was the due of a chieftain, she headed directly to the local lord's castle to claim the expected hospitality. The Lord of Howth not only refused to unlock the gates to his castle, but had his servants report that he was in the middle of dinner and that Grace should be on her way. Understandably furious, she stormed back to her ship, on the way kidnapping the lord's grandson and heir. The lord tried to buy the boy back, but Grace wasn't interested in money: she demanded that Lord Howth swear always to leave his castle gates unlocked and set an extra place at the table for anyone who wanted to stop by. The lord gave Grace a ring as a sign of his agreement, she returned his grandson, and even today the inhabitants of Howth Castle keep an extra chair and setting at the table.

After Hen's Castle passed to Dónal's cousin, Grace settled in a castle on Clare Island. Small and sheltered, with fewer than one hundred inhabitants and rarely noticed by passing ships, the island offered a fine view of the bay and the coming and going of potential prey. Controlling at least three galleys and several smaller boats, Grace continued her piracy and protection business. Here, one Saint Brigid's Day [as the story goes] she was on a pilgrimage at the holy well on the island when she learned of a ship that had foundered in bad weather near Achill Head. Grace and her crew headed out into the gale to find what booty they could, and in the wreckage she found a young man—Hugh de Lacy, a wealthy son of a merchant. Like so much plunder, Grace brought him back with her to Clare Island, but unlike most pirate kidnappings, this couple fell in love. However, their love was not to outlast the season. Not long after the gale, while Hugh was hunting deer in Achill, he was murdered by the

MacMahons of neighboring Donna Castle. Heartbroken, Grace waited and watched from her castle until the MacMahons left on pilgrimage themselves, to the nearby island of Caher. Then she struck, first capturing their boats and so stranding them on the island. She killed the man she suspected was responsible for Hugh's death; then she sailed off to seize the MacMahon castle.

Still in her thirties, Grace had her fourth child, a blue-eyed, blond-haired boy she named Theobald, giving birth to the boy on board her ship. The next day, the vessel was attacked by Algerian pirates, and Grace remained belowdecks with her newborn while the fighting raged on the deck above. Her crew was close to losing the skirmish when the captain came and asked her to come up and motivate her men to fight. "May you be seven times worse off this day twelve months," she shouted as she ran onto the deck, "who cannot do without me for one day!" Her crew rallied and overcame the Algerians. Theobald came to be known as Tibbot-ne-Long, or Tibód-na-Long, meaning Toby of the Ships.

By 1567, Grace had once again remarried, to the chieftain Richard Bourke, known as Richard-an-Iarainn [Iron Richard], and moved to his castle on Clew Bay. This was a good marriage for Grace—Richard was a prominent and powerful man who owned fertile lands with sheltered harbors. Grace brought a dowry of cattle and horses to the marriage, with the assurance that she would have the equivalent returned if he died or they divorced. By some accounts a trial marriage, with Grace locking Richard out of his own castle after a year, the couple in any case found some appeal in each other, as they were together

until Richard died of natural causes in 1583, when Grace was in her early fifties. Remembering how she had been denied her inheritance after her first marriage, Grace immediately claimed one-third of Richard's land.

In the spring of 1577, while heading south to Munster on a pirate raid, Grace was caught and imprisoned for a year and a half in Limerick, and then transferred to Dublin Castle. Only famous and politically important prisoners were kept in the castle—although it's doubtful that the transfer flattered her. Death was almost always the only way out of Dublin Castle, and indeed the three men captured with Grace were all executed, but in early 1579, for unrecorded reasons, she was freed.

Through the later years of her career, Grace and her clan repeatedly locked horns with Richard Bingham, the English governor of Connaught. Bingham's men killed her son Owen and imprisoned her son Tibbot for more than a year. Grace was soon in open rebellion against Bingham, and fearing her wealth, power, and hundreds of mercenaries, the governor ordered her capture. Bingham built a gallows, clearly meant for Grace, but her son-in-law managed to secure her release with a pledge of loyalty which he reversed, joining Grace's rebellion immediately on her release. The feud kept on, and Bingham's naval forces made it difficult for Grace to earn a living in the seafaring manner to which she was accustomed. Weary of this, at age sixty-three, Grace went over Bingham's head, sailing to London to seek audience with Queen Elizabeth. Even recognized Irish chieftains rarely were granted royal audiences, but in the summer of 1593—a season that saw an outbreak of the plague—Grace was permitted to make her case to Elizabeth. Barefoot and dressed in Irish clothing, Grace explained to the queen that the constant dis-

cord in Ireland required that she keep her own army to protect her clan, and also recounted her twice-widowed state and inability to inherit her husbands' property—a situation the queen found unfair. She wasn't asking for much: a maintenance for the little time she had left to live, and the release of her son Tibbot from Bingham. Oh, and permission to attack with sword and fire all the queen's enemies. Like Grace, Queen Elizabeth had outlived the expected lifespan for a woman of her time. She was intelligent, popular, and bullying—it's easy to imagine the two of them getting along. The queen wrote to Bingham and told him to leave Grace and her fleet alone, and to release her son. Although Bingham did not immediately stop harassing her, in 1595 he was arrested for unrelated charges, and Grace was finally free of him. She returned to making the living she knew best, raiding ships far north and south, and was still leading pirate raids from the decks of her ships as late as the summer of 1601. She died sometime around 1603, most likely at her Carraigahowley Castle.

1775

American Colonies

Fanny Campbell

Fanny Campbell

Fanny Campbell was tough—she's supposed to have killed a wildcat when she was just a girl—but it was love that led her to the pirate life. As a young woman, she rescued her beau from a Cuban prison and then turned to attacking British ships at the start of the American Revolution, seizing booty and making mischief on behalf of the soon-to-be-independent colonies.

Fanny grew up in Lynn, Massachusetts, an agricultural community a few miles northeast of Boston. She fell in love with the boy next door, William Lovell, a merchant sailor who taught her how to handle a ship. The pair got engaged, but before they could marry, William was sent to sea on a two-year voyage to South America and the West Indies on the merchant ship *Royal Kent*. When pirates took the *Royal Kent* near Cuba, William fought bravely and was wounded in battle. The pirates kidnapped sailors from the merchant ship to

replace crewmembers killed in the fight, and William was one of them. While the pirate ship was docked in Cuba, he and two other men, Henry Breed and Jack Herbert, escaped, but the trio was soon arrested for "looking suspicious" and charged with piracy. After six months in jail William finally had his day in court. The trial was a mockery—there was no evidence of piracy, yet he was found guilty and sent back to prison with his companions.

After six more months in the Cuban jail, Jack Herbert managed to escape and stow away on an American ship headed for Boston. Before Jack fled Cuba, William gave his friend a note to give to Fanny, letting her know what had happened and reassuring her that he was, at least, alive.

In the year that William was gone, British navy Captain Robert Burnet made a play for Fanny's affections but she rejected him, staying true to her betrothed. When she got word from Jack Herbert of William's predicament she knew just what to do. Adopting the name

"Channing," dressed as a man, and using the sea-knowledge William taught her, she headed to Boston Harbor and signed on as second officer aboard the *Constance*, a merchant brig on its way to England via Cuba. Help was on the way.

The captain of the *Constance*, a Captain Brownless, was cruel and hated, and the first mate cared not at all what happened to the ship or its crew. Fanny craftily took advantage of the situation a week into their voyage. "He's going to have us all pressed by the navy when we get to England!" she warned her shipmates [including Jack Herbert, who had also signed aboard but had no idea that "Channing" might be Fanny]. Tensions had been simmering among the crew for some time, and the rumor was enough to spark a mutiny, led by Fanny. This officially made the crew outlaws, and their first order of business was to elect the "man" who'd led the revolt as

their new captain. Fanny, still in disguise and now with a ship full of pirates at her command, kept course for Cuba, and for William.

En route to the island they encountered a British barque, the *George,* which Fanny and her crew captured despite the *George*'s superior firepower. A few nights later, with both ships under her command, Fanny sailed into Havana Bay. She sent Herbert and eight other men to row to the massive, Spanish-built stone fortress where William was being held. Killing four Cuban guards, the pirates freed William and ten other Americans and rowed them all back to the ship.

William was summoned to the captain's cabin, where he discovered that the brave pirate captain who freed him was his own fiancée, Fanny. The two managed to keep this a secret from the rest of the crew—though it couldn't have been easy to play it cool after everything that had happened—and pirate life went on. The *Constance* and the *George* headed back out to sea, where they soon captured another ship, a British merchantman carrying not only booty but interesting news: the Revolution had begun.

This stroke of good luck meant that Fanny and her crew could go legal as privateers—pirates in service of the government—and attack British ships. Suddenly they were patriots, and Fanny's fleet was now one of private warships rather than pirate marauders. On their first day as privateers they captured a British sloop that, according to legend, was captained by none other than Robert

Burnet, who recognized Fanny but for whatever reason kept Captain Channing's identify to himself.

When Fanny sailed the *George* and the *Constance* back to Massachusetts, she tried at first to put in at Boston Harbor but found it was controlled by the British. Instead, she turned the ships to Marblehead, Massachusetts, where the crew could file the papers to legally become privateers. Once ashore, Fanny and William returned to Lynn for paperwork of a different kind—to be married. William continued as a privateer throughout the Revolution, but Fanny remained ashore with the start of what was to become a large family.

1680s

Arabian Sea

Anonymous Indian Pirate Queen

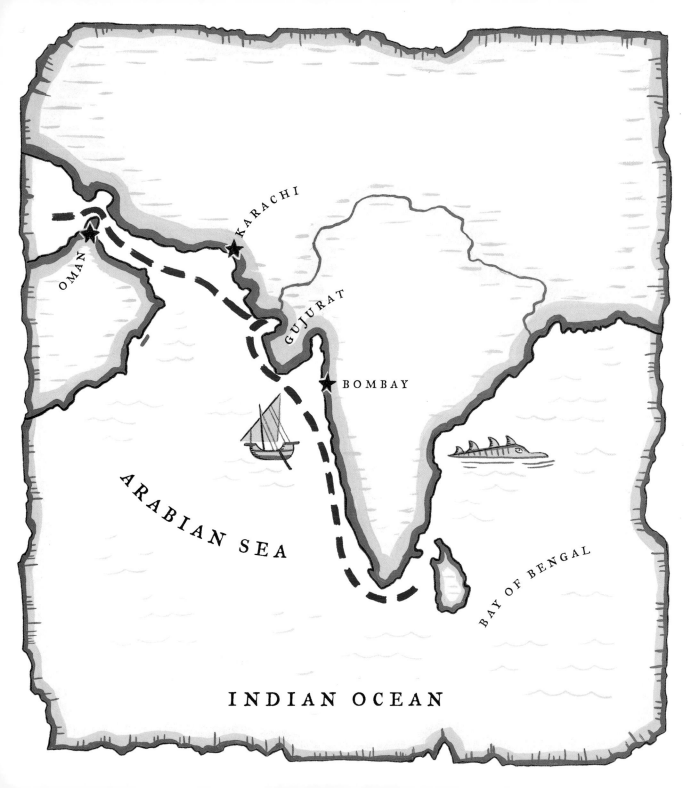

KARACHI

OMAN

GUJURAT

BOMBAY

ARABIAN SEA

BAY OF BENGAL

INDIAN OCEAN

Anonymous Indian Pirate Queen

Pirates infested the seas around the Indian subcontinent for centuries—Pliny the Elder complained about pirates attacking ships along the Red Sea route to India in the first century A.D. The sixteenth to eighteenth centuries were the Golden Age of Piracy in India and Europe. Sailing Indian waters between England and her colonies, ships carrying exotic goods such as tea and spices made excellent targets; Indian and European pirates alike availed themselves of the easy booty.

One of the most fascinating Indian pirates is, unfortunately, anonymous. Her name was never recorded, and although she may never have set foot on a pirate ship herself, she commanded an enormous fleet—perhaps the only Indian woman in history to do so. She governed the province and town of Kutch [now Bhuj], India, having been chosen because her people felt that a woman, being compliant

and gentle by nature, was more likely to listen to their complaints and grievances. But she ruled with such force and intimidation that the rulers of neighboring states lived in fear, and left her in peace.

The crews of her pirate fleet were mostly Sanjanians, who came from an area approximately ninety miles north of Bombay. Her swift, streamlined ships—perfect for piracy—prowled the entire western coast of India and beyond, from the Strait of Hormuz to the Gulf of Mannar, often bringing their captives to the city of Biet to be ransomed. Although they were usually outgunned, the queen's men outnumbered their prey and swarmed aboard before their victims had a chance to defend themselves. If they did draw fire, the pirates sped away, and were rarely captured.

In 1684, the queen's pirates made a capture that would earn her a place in the history books. After an all-day chase from early in the morning until four in the afternoon, her men captured a ten-gun English ship, *Merchant's Delight,* and the trader's smaller, four-gun companion vessel. The pirates sailed the *Merchant's Delight* in the direction of Aramra, a seaport in Gujarat. When they came close to shore, they offered the traditional pirate salute, firing a cannon in honor of their families and country. Unbeknownst to the pirates, the ship's captain, Edward Say, had hidden fifteen hundred Venetian gold coins in his guns, and the salute blasted about seven hundred of them out to sea. Appraised of the contents of the ship's list, the queen demanded that Say—barefoot, bareheaded, half his hand mangled in the attack by her men—account for the missing booty. Through an interpreter she questioned him about the missing coins, demanding to know who had taken them. Say told her the truth, but the story seemed so unlikely she was sure he was lying and that he had the gold hidden away for himself. She informed him that she would never let

him see England again and he would have nothing but salt water to drink for the rest of his days. Regardless, Say kept to his story.

But the queen wasn't going to let the coins go that easily. She recalled a Portuguese priest, whom she had captured earlier, and his explanation of his reverence for several foot-high statues of saints and the Virgin Mary—now in her possession. Not knowing any other Europeans, she assumed that all were as devout as this priest, and she resolved to test the captain using the statues. Kiss them, she demanded, expecting Say would be too terrified to do so if he was lying. Say, neither lying nor Catholic, had no trouble in kissing the statues. The queen kept him a few more days before deciding that he probably was telling the truth. In the end, she returned the *Merchant's Delight* and gave Say twelve pints of wheat as provisions for his voyage. Instead, for reasons that are not clear, Say embarked on an Arab ship on its way to Muscat, on the Gulf of Oman, bringing with him stories of India's only pirate queen.

The Classic Pirate Lifestyle

Victuals

While aboard ship, pirates usually ate two meals a day, one in the morning and one in the late afternoon. They ate more or less the same food at both meals, which were all-you-can-eat when supplies were plentiful. Captains ate with the crew. Some ships had cooks, who were chosen not for their culinary flair but because they'd lost a hand or a foot and now weren't so nimble at climbing ropes.

Pirates kept chickens, goats, pigs, cows, and other animals on board, live, which they'd slaughter on deck. In lean times, they might cast a hungry eye on any pets on board: dogs, cats, parrots, monkeys, penguins. Rats were fair game, too. Turtles, which could weigh more than a hundred pounds and be kept alive on board for several weeks, were also popular, and had the added appeal of being fun to catch. Pirates might flip them on their backs on land; harpoon them at sea; or reel them in using remoras tied to ropes, once the remoras had suckered themselves to the turtles' shells.

Fishing off the ship might yield a catch of shark, dolphin, porpoise, or other fish. And of course pirates stole food—whatever looked good—from the ships and towns they raided. Soups and stews with flexible ingredients were standbys of pirate cuisine. The following is an approximation, adapted from an antique recipe, of what might go into an ideal pirate turtle soup.

Pirate Turtle Soup

1 turtle [approx. 25 lbs.]
fresh water to cover
salt and pepper [1/2 cup each or to taste]
available vegetables [recommend 15 lbs. potatoes,
    celery, carrots]
several onions
1 head garlic
sage, parsley [1/2 cup each or to taste], or available seasonings
6 lbs. clams [optional]
3 cups oil [or available fat]

Bring water to a boil with turtle and clams. Chop vegetables and onions. Peel and chop garlic. Remove turtle from pot when tender. Cut in bite-sized pieces, return to pot. Add potatoes, carrots, celery, onions, garlic, and seasonings. Add oil and stir. Cook till vegetables are tender. Serve with ship's biscuit. Feeds twenty hungry pirates.

Grog

Pirates loved rum, but they also loved wine, beer, and a boozy punch called "sangaree" [what's now known as sangria], and all of it in huge quantities—they were generally allowed to have as much to drink as they wanted, all day long. The rum went down straight or in one of an array of cocktails, enjoyed but not necessarily invented by pirates, including the West Indian "bumboo" [rum, water, sugar, and nutmeg] and "grog" [rum and water, sometimes with spices and lemon]. A "flipp" was beer mixed with spirits and sugar, and a "rumfustian" was a fierce concoction of beer, gin, sherry, cinnamon, and nutmeg, served hot. Anything beat the taste of the nasty, but necessary, barrel-stored water.

Flogging

At the beginning of each voyage, pirate captains might write a formal contract, called the ship's articles, which was signed by all hands, and bound them to certain conduct. Even crews without such articles knew clearly what was allowed and what wasn't, and knew how they'd be punished if they stepped over the line. The punishments inflicted by pirates on each other were generally much more merciful than those suffered by their victims, or those that the royal navies—which many pirates were fleeing—inflicted on the pirates and even their own sailors. The various punishments included being:

FLOGGED: Whipped with a cat-o'-nine-tails, a punishment used by the navies and pirates alike. A pirate might be whipped for smoking in the hold without a safety cap on her pipe, carrying a candle without a lantern, or snapping her gun—all forbidden in the interest of preventing fires in a wooden ship miles from shore. Flogging was also the punishment on some ships for beating another pirate.

WOOLDED: Tying a prisoner to a mast and tightening cords around his head. Used to extract information rather than to kill.

QUARTERED: Being pulled apart by having one's limbs attached to objects—horses, levers, etc.—each moving in a separate direction. Generally not done at sea, and generally too much trouble for pirates to bother with, but Cheng I Sao is said to have had an occasional victim quartered.

KEELHAULED: A punishment employed on merchant and naval vessels in which a sailor or captive was dragged underwater from one end of the keel to the other. Seldom employed by pirates, and any who did generally learned it in the navy.

MAROONED: Left on land to fend for one's self, often on a small desert island, with only a bit of water, a gun, powder, and some shot. A favorite punishment for untrustworthy pirates who tried to desert their crews or steal more than a certain amount of booty from their shipmates.

HANGED: Breaking of one's neck at the end of a rope. The preferred way to go, if you had to, since it was quick and relatively painless. A punishment often suffered by pirates at the hands of authorities.

FORCED TO WALK THE PLANK: Of all the ways of dying on a pirate ship, this is the most classic. The victim, hands tied, maybe a chain around her ankles, is forced at the point of a cutlass to step out on the shaky wooden board. Pirates in headscarves chortle from the deck, passing around a bottle of rum, as the victim is forced to take one step out—away from the ship—the wood trembles—a parrot says something witty—another step, and the victim falls into the water and is dragged down to her death. But [except for Sadie the Goat] it never happened. Pirates didn't use planks. Anyone who went overboard was usually already dead.

Booty

Pirate crews divided their booty democratically. Most pirate captains received one and a half shares of all prizes while the quartermaster [who was in charge of dividing the loot], carpenter, boatswain, and gunner earned one and a quarter shares, the rest a single share. The pirates then immediately squandered their riches, rather than burying them in sea chests under palm trees.

Before paying out, the quartermaster set some aside for a fund to pay reparations to the injured, such as for the loss of a limb, eye, or finger. Sometimes pirates would get just as much for losing a wooden leg as a real one, as wooden legs were so hard to come by. If a pirate broke the rules and wasn't flogged or otherwise physically punished, she was fined and a share of her booty was forfeit.

Privacy

The typical pirate ship was chaotic and crowded. Areas below deck were dimly lit and strewn with piles of cargo crates and provision barrels, with only about five feet to stand up in. Canvas hammocks, each about three by six feet, hung only a few inches from each other. The crew ate and slept at all hours, when they weren't drinking, singing, card playing, sewing, or involved in other pirate activities. With this going on a female pirate passing as a man was easily able to find a hidden corner or a distraction to protect her identity if she needed to change clothes. As difficult as it is to imagine pirates being

bashful, respecting privacy was a necessary survival skill on a crowded ship, and they tended to keep a certain mental and physical distance from each other when possible.

On most ships, men urinated while standing on ledges off the ship. Women serving secretly in the military or on ships have used short tubes and other gadgets to let them pee standing up [Mrs. Christian Davies, a dragoon in the Spanish War of Succession, used a silver tube to urinate, a trick she learned from another female soldier; a German contemporary of Mary Read's used a leather-covered horn, which she kept fastened to her body]. Even with special devices, a disguised pirate might time her trips to the head to minimize chance of discovery, at night or when her shipmates were otherwise occupied.

The design of some ships allowed for the construction of makeshift "seats of easement," planks at the edge of the ship with holes cut in them, to sit on as in an outhouse, and these were usually as out of sight as possible. Some ships had heads indoors, with chutes sending the waste to the sea, and on smaller ships without heads sailors just perched on the forechains.

The poor pirate diet and hard labor of shipboard life may have stopped some of the women pirates from menstruating.

Fashion

If a female pirate was trying to pass as a man, she dressed like a man. For Anne Bonny and Mary Read, for instance, this means they would have worn short blue coats over loose checkered shirts, long baggy pants of striped canvas, and red kerchiefs around their necks. Pirates were responsible for providing their own clothing, and many came aboard with just the clothes they were wearing. Anne and Mary could have worn the same pants and shirts, mending them as necessary, for a year without anyone thinking it was odd. No one changed into pajamas before going to bed, and pirates rarely bathed or went swimming.

Pirates had deep tans from long exposure to the sun, and coarse skin from the wind and salt water. Their arms were muscular from the hard labor of shipboard life, and they earned many cuts, scars, and bruises from handling the ropes and chains of the ship— and a few more in the course of raiding ships. If their hair was of any length, it was matted by the sea wind, and pirates male and female preferred to keep their hair short or in a ponytail.

Frigging

Pirates, like other sailors, were reluctant to have women aboard—one crew's articles went so far as to declare that any pirate who smuggled a woman onto their ship would be executed—because they considered their presence disruptive. Some ships even refused to take young boys aboard. But whatever happened on shore, at the brothels and in the taverns, was less restricted.

Some captains tried to govern their men's behavior toward female captives. The articles of one ship stated that, should a pirate meet "with a prudent Woman, that Man that offers to meddle with her, without her Consent, shall suffer present Death." But such rules could sometimes be hard to enforce.

Further Reading

My research and interest in pirates was fueled by easy access to the hundreds of books on seafaring in the collections of the New York Public Library and Columbia University. Some of the following books are easier to track down than others. I hope that anyone inspired to sail further into the ocean of pirate books will find this selective list helpful and encouraging.

Good Places to Start

☞ Carse, Robert. *The Age of Piracy.* New York: Rinehart & Company, 1957.

☞ Cordingly, David. *Under the Black Flag: The Romance and the Reality of Life Among the Pirates.* New York: Random House, 1995.

☞ Cordingly, David, ed. *Pirates: Terror on the High Seas from the Caribbean to the South China Sea.* North Dighton, Mass: JG Press, 1998.

☞ Ellms, Charles. *The Pirates' Own Book: Authentic Narratives of the Most Celebrated Sea Robbers.* Mineola, New York: Dover Publications, 1993. Originally published by Samuel N. Dickinson, 1837.

☞ Esquemeling, John [Exquemelin, A. O.]. *The Buccaneers of America.* First English edition published in 1685.

☞ Gosse, Philip. *The Pirates' Who's Who, Giving Particulars of the Lives & Deaths of the Pirates and Buccaneers.* London: Dulau Company, 1924.

⌘ Rediker, Marcus. *Between the Devil and the Deep Blue Sea: Merchant Seamen, Pirates, and the Anglo-American Maritime World*, 1700–1750. New York: Cambridge University Press, 1987.

⌘ Stanley, Jo, ed. *Bold in Her Breeches: Women Pirates Across the Ages*. San Francisco: Pandora, 1995.

⌘ Winston, Alexander. *No Man Knows My Grave: Sir Henry Morgan, Captain William Kidd, Captain Woodes Rogers in the Great Age of Privateers and Pirates*, 1665–1715. Boston: Houghton Mifflin Company, 1969.

⌘ Woodbury, George. *The Great Days of Piracy in the West Indies*. New York: W. W. Norton & Company, 1951.

By Pirate
Sadie the Goat

⌘ Asbury, Herbert. *The Gangs of New York: An Informal History of the Underworld*. Garden City, New York: Garden City Publishing Co., 1928.

⌘ Crapsey, Edward. *The Nether Side of New York; or, the Vice, Crime, and Poverty of the Great Metropolis*. New York: Sheldon & Company, 1872.

⌘ Sante, Luc. *Low Life: Lures and Snares of Old New York*. New York: Vintage Books, 1992.

Cheng I Sao

⌘ Glasspoole, Richard. *Mr. Glasspoole and the Chinese Pirates*. London: The Golden Cockerel Press, 1935.

⌘ Murray, Dian H. *Pirates of the South China Coast*, 1790–1810. Stanford: Stanford University Press, 1987.

Alphild

🖎 Saxo Grammaticus. *The First Nine Books of the Danish History.*
   [Thirteenth century A.D.]

Rachel Wall

🖎 Williams, Daniel E. *Pillars of Salt: An Anthology of Early
   American Criminal Narratives.* Madison, Wisconsin: Madison
   House, 1993.

Mary Read and Anne Bonny

🖎 Johnson, Charles. *A General History of the Pyrates* .... London:
   T. Warner, 1724.
🖎 *The Tryals of Captain John Rackham and other Pirates* .... Jamaica:
   Robert Baldwin, 1721.

Charlotte de Berry

🖎 Yolen, Jane H. *Pirates in Petticoats.* New York: Van Rees Press, 1963.

Lai Choi San

🖎 Lilius, Aleko E. *I Sailed with Chinese Pirates.* London:
   Arrowsmith, 1930.

Lady Mary Killigrew

🖎 Williams, Neville. *Captains Outrageous: Seven Centuries of Piracy.*
   London: Barrie and Rockliff, 1961.
🖎 Yolen, Jane H. *Pirates in Petticoats.* New York: Van Rees Press,
   1963.

Grace O'Malley (Granuaile)

☞ Chambers, Anne. *Granuaile: The Life and Times of Grace O'Malley c. 1530–1603.* Dublin: Wolfhound Press, originally published 1979, second edition 1988.

Fanny Campbell

☞ De Pauw, Linda Grant. *Seafaring Women.* Boston: Houghton Mifflin, 1982.

☞ Snow, Edward Rowe. *True Tales of Pirates and Their Gold.* New York: Dodd, Mead & Company, 1953.

Anonymous Indian Pirate Queen

☞ Saletore, Rajaram Narayan. *Indian Pirates: From the Earliest Times to the Present Day.* Delhi: Concept Publishing Company, 1978.

Booty

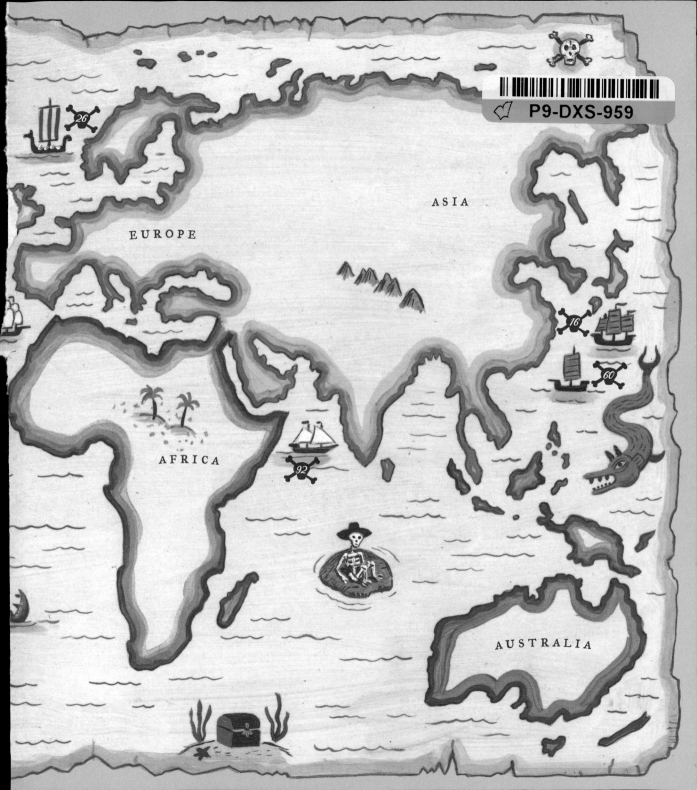

P9-DXS-959